AV

HOT JETS

HOT JETS

SUPERSONIC FIGHTERS OF USAF

JERRY SCUTTS

HAMLYN

First published in 1989 by
The Hamlyn Publishing Group,
a division of The Octopus Publishing Group Ltd
Michelin House, 81 Fulham Road, London SW3 6RB

© The Hamlyn Publishing Group 1989

Colour artworks: © Pilot Press, Octopus Books Ltd

Typeset by MS Filmsetting Limited, Frome, Somerset

Printed and bound in Spain by Gráficas Estella, S.A. Navarra.

ISBN 0600 564 35 5

Series Editor: Len Cacutt
Art Editor: James Hughes
Designer: Brian Folkard
Production: Hilary Stephens

Contents

Strike Fighter Requirement

In the late 1950s the USAF laid plans for a future strike fighter, one which would follow on from the Century series of interceptors then entering service. Known as the Tactical Fighter Experimental (TFX) this new specification was far-reaching but would not, it was estimated, come together as actual hardware until the mid-1960s at the earliest. In the meantime it was necessary for the Air Force to acquire a new fighter that would equip the squadrons of Tactical Air Command in a far shorter timescale.

Air Force chiefs saw, by the early part of the

Below: F-4D Phantom of the Air Force Reserve's 465th Tactical Fighter Squadron, 507th TFG at Tinker AFB, Oklahoma in 'F-16' style camouflage.

decade, that there really was only one fighter that would fulfill the need: the Navy had in 1958 flown the prototype of the McDonnell Douglas F-4 Phantom II and the sparkling performance of this twin-engined, two-seat monster looked set to match anything in the skies, Western or Eastern. Traditionally preferring to order aircraft tailor-made to its own missions, the Air Force saw that far from being on schedule, TFX was beginning to lag seriously, mainly as a result of a desire to produce an 'all singing, all dancing' airplane that would do the job of a number of others and be equally adaptable to launching from a carrier and taking off from 2000 yards of concrete. It was a tall order that would take much time to meet.

Overcoming their reluctance in buying an aircraft designed for another service, the Air Force evaluated the F-4B in 1963. They found that the Phantom did everything and more that the brochure said it would. Modification to Air Force requirements would not take very long, nor would there be a large hole in the purse, especially if changes were kept to a minimum.

The die was cast: USAF F-4s would be built as soon as the parent company could initiate the production changes 'on the line'. In the meantime, the USAF borrowed 30 Navy F-4Bs in order to establish a training program on the

new type as soon as possible. These entered service at McDill Air Force Base in November 1963, a timely action that would have far-reaching effects and soon reveal the soundness of the decision.

In a period about to undergo an upheaval which would change the course of military planning out of all recognition, the Phantom was, like all other first-line fighters and bombers in the US inventory, expected to be a couple of steps ahead of what the Soviet Union could come up with – just in case. For good as the fighters of the 1950s had been, technological progress had been rapid since the end of World War II. It was well known that the Eastern bloc had many excellent aircraft, and plenty of them. The Korean War had shown that, fortunately, pilot training and some would say dedication to the art of the fighter pilot, had made the difference in air-to-air combat

Above: One of the Air Guard's RF-4C Phantoms in 'wraparound' camouflage streams its braking 'chute after landing.

7

with Russia's best, flown by her North Korea customer.

The First Jet-versus-Jet Combats

While Korea saw the first jet-versus-jet combats in history, the tactics used were largely those of the previous world war. In a scant five years, marked by the 'swords into plough-shares' attitudes of governments, no great strides had been made. The propulsive power of fighter aircraft had changed so that jet engines were rapidly taking over from the piston engine in those air forces willing and able to bear the cost of development and procure-

ment. Both East and West had gained much from the spoils of war and a good deal of the technical advances made by Germany were adapted and refined; Britain's know-how also carved a significant niche in the post war military aircraft scene, building on her early lead in jet propulsion. A little slower than the Americans in also seeing the potential of the swept wing for a full-blown production jet fighter, the RAF and Royal Navy persisted with straight wing jets for a considerable time. As events were to show, an unfortunate 'own goal' was to send examples of the Rolls-Royce Nene engine to Britain's erstwhile World War

Opposite: A USAF F-4C blasts off from a base in Thailand in mid-1966. The immense width of the air intake trunking can well be seen.

Below: An RF-4C of the 38th TRS, 26th Tac Recon Wing at Zweibrucken, West Germany.

II ally, whereupon Russian engineers rapidly caught up with production methods and soon began to produce their own jet engines in quantity.

Thus it was that the Russians were able to supply North Korea with ample numbers of swept-wing MiG-15 fighters; in service by the middle of the conflict, the agile MiG was matched by only one type in United Nations'

Service, the F-86 Sabre. Without exception, every other jet type on either side was of the earlier, straight-winged variety. Clearly the North Koreans had the potential to sweep the UN from the skies.

As history was to record the USAF Sabre wings denied the communists that victory and turned in a kill ratio of more than three to one. For the Air Force, the jet fighter 'learning

Below: Bright tail trim on RF-4C Phantom of the 62nd TRS, 363rd TRW, one of many units which still fly the recon version.

curve' had begun to climb – but it is true to say that most NKAF pilots lacked the skill to stretch the American curriculum very far. Many tactics were expedient and tailored to match the ad hoc deployment of the MiG formations which flew under ground control for most of the time, and often failed to press home any advantages they had. The US Sabre pilots observed some exceptions – the skillful, aggressive 'honchos' who had obviously spent plenty of hours in a fighter cockpit and knew their business. These men, undoubtedly Russian as well as North Korean, were seemingly in short supply – the majority of MiG pilots did not show many 'gung ho' qualities and a lot more of them than necessary were shot down by a fighter that was usually at the limits of its fuel and was more lightly armed. Indeed, merely the thought of taking on the tough Americans was enough for some MiG pilots to bail out without firing a shot.

When the Korean war ended, the USAF determined that it would not be found wanting in any future conflict (as it had when the war began in 1950) and major programs were implemented to build new and better fighters armed not only with guns but a whole array of air-to-air and air-to-ground missiles. And as these programs came to fruition the USAF remained one of the most potent forces of its kind in the world.

But good as the fighters of the mid 1950s were, they still did not stretch the young fight-

er pilots with an exhaustive round of gunnery and fighter tactics. In a period when many potentially lethal weapons were tested and put into production, the trade of the fighter pilot was over-shadowed by the Bomb and the Cold War. Looking back, the threat seemed always to be with us.

Not 'If' but 'When'

Gradually the Iron Curtain extended and even though the threat was far more tangible than overt action on the part of the USSR, few

Above: The Navy recon Phantom was designated RF-4B and this view shows four holding tight formation for the C-130 camera ship. In Marine Corps hands, the Phantoms are from VMFP-3.

Above: Another AFRES Phantom from the 465th TFS, this time a D model. The aircraft carries a standard centreline fuel tank and small practise bomb dispensers on the pylons. Reserve squadrons, the 'weekend warriors', provide a high number of trained crews as part of the Air Force.

service chiefs in the West would then have advocated pruning military budgets and reducing preparedness for whatever might lay in the future. World War III scenarios were thick in the files – at times it seemed not a case of 'if', but 'when' the world would blow apart as East/West tension neared breaking point.

Getting on with his job, the American fighter pilot traded his Sabre (with regrets) and passed perhaps to the latest spearhead designed to follow up if there was anything left for him to do after the B-47s and B-58s had returned to base. In the fulness of time the single-seat exponent traded the F-84F (with few regrets, thankful that he had at least not been asked to drop the Big One from it) and went onto a Super Sabre, Voodoo or Starfighter – the popularly dubbed 'missile with a man in it'. Missiles were the coming thing and there were doubts, as these got bigger and

better, that soon mere mortals would not be needed to fly airplanes anymore. Air combat? It was rapidly becoming a thing of the past. Along with the built-in gun, air action between fighters was being relegated to history, at least for any future generation of fighters – which had, ever since World War II, been thought of primarily as tools to intercept enemy bombers.

And, so the train of official thought went, even if fighters did get to grips with each other, the fight would not be the close-in affair that it was in World War II. Long-range targets only needed a missile or two and soon there would be little need for the fighter pilot even to see the target, such were the advances being made in radars.

As things transpired, few Americans got the chance to use an F-100, F-101, F-102 or F-104 to anywhere near its limits. Few regular fighter pilots, save for those who scaled the shining pinnacles and were selected for the Skyblazers or the Thunderbirds aerobatic teams, knew what their aircraft could do, particularly against enemy fighters. Month in, year out, the US fighter pilot did his routine job by the book.

Ready with the Ultimate Weapon

In peaceful skies from Nevada to Norfolk and Ramstein to Rekyavik the brightly trimmed silver fighters of Tactical Air Command, of USAF Europe and Pacific Air Forces patrolled

The F-104's widely
acclaimed performance made it
an attractive buy for overseas
air forces. This early example
lacks the wingtip fuel tanks.

and maintained a presence. NATO's vast land mass was assured that if the worst ever happened US fast jets were ready to defend democracy, many of them able to tote the Ultimate Weapon if the need arose. Peace was maintained through the 1950s and into the next decade, although in some parts of the world, the fact was debatable. But so far as East and West were concerned, the worst did not happen.

As the next decade dawned, little had really changed. The US fighter pilot still swept the skies alone, taking on board with him a gradually increasing amount of electronic gadgetry that, in theory, made his job easier; it meant more hours in the classroom and countless

Left: Five Grand. Decorated with the flags of buyer nations the 5,000th F-4 built screams over St Louis during March 1978. An E model, it was sold to Turkey.

Below: From '58 to '88. Well polished F-4E of the 131st TFW, Missouri Air Guard, 68–388 also got a MiG kill in Vietnam. A second red star has since appeared.

hours of practice. Weapons training on the ranges sharpened his edge. He was still able to hack it.

Then came the Phantom. It was certainly not the first time that two men had sat in a fighter; when they had it had usually been with a set of priorities, like radar operating and navigating. But in 1963, the cockpit had simply become too cluttered with equipment to navigate, search and guide the weapons system, and the fighter pilot found that he was no longer alone. Should the crunch ever come he would be far too busy merely flying the ship to divert his attention to doing what a fighter pilot is supposed to do – or so the theory went. The Navy had designed the F-4 to take a crew of two, and so would the Air Force.

Whereas the Navy decided against it, the Air Force went for a dual control aircraft, so that in the event of the pilot being incapacitated, the back-seat man could fly home. He was in fact the pilot. It was the man in the front who was now the Aircraft Commander. To many, it was a strange set-up. Almost eerie. What would this pilot, this 'guy in the back' actually do on missions?

Fighter pilots were traditionally loners. There was nothing wrong with that – they liked it that way. Small wonder that some individuals selected to fly the Phantom cast wistful glances over their shoulders to Korea and even World War II: in neither of those wars had there been a need for more than one cockpit on a fighter. A man went out and did his job. Alone. Just like it always had been. Was all that tradition to be swept away?

'A Very Low-Key Affair'

Below: F-105D Thunderchief of the 354th TFS named 'The Ripper' en route home from a North Vietnamese target with empty bomb racks.

Then, just as the Air Force Phantom numbers were building and the training program getting into its stride, war errupted in a small country on the other side of the world that most Americans had hardly even heard of. At first it was a very low-key affair, a series of small skirmishes.

But as it turned out, the war did not take too long to turn into something more serious. Both the Navy and the Air Force began flying strike missions into North Vietnam, tentatively at first, to give Ho Chi Minh's regime ample opportunity to stop insurgency south of the Demilitarised Zone. There was no response.

Tactical Air Command began sending its fighter bombers to Thailand, the mightly F-105 Thunderchief taking on an increasing share of the action. The B-57 and F-100 had clearly passed their prime when it came to laying iron bombs on heavily defended targets and the supersonic 'Thud', despite a poor service record at home, began to show its mettle.

Whatever the level of combat, TAC commanders knew that flying in a war zone had to add impetus to a fighter pilot's skills, the best of whom had never stopped training in order to keep on top. On a regular basis, squadrons were rotated into Thailand in order to find out if they could be used to any good effect to end the war. But having been designed for a conflict entirely different to the one they found in Vietnam, only a handful of fighters did get to fly missions reguarly.

Some aircraft without a great load-carrying capacity could not be fitted into what was a predominantly ground-attack war. The F-102 Delta Dagger saw limited deployment in the air defense role from Thai bases and it did fly some escort sorties for B-52 missions. But as the North Vietnamese Air Force rarely ventured into South Vietnam, the air defense role was hardly necessary.

The Starfighter was absorbed into mission planning for a couple of limited periods, although once again its performance and load-carrying capability did not match the current requirements. By the early 1960s the day of the

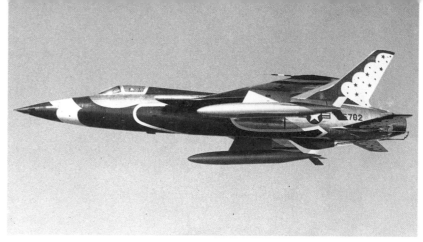

McDonnell Voodoo as an interceptor had all but passed and instead the RF-101 found a useful role in the exacting and highly dangerous task of photo reconnaissance.

That left the F-100 and F-105 as the remaining members of the Century series family, and both became TAC stars in the war that escalated into a long-drawn-out slogging match, albeit on different sides of the fence. Having been the first true supersonic (Mach 1) fighter in USAF inventory, the Super Sabre was deadly efficient in the ground-attack role – indeed it was destined to fly more sorties in the course of the Vietnam war than any other Air Force type.

F-105s Hunting Ground

North Vietnam was the hunting ground of the F-105. Tough, rugged and large enough to

Above: The earlier model F-105B was used by the USAF aerobatic team for six shows in 1964 before the Thunderbirds relinquished it for the F-100D. Nine aircraft were modified for the team and the majority later served in ANG units.

F-4Ds of the 8th TFW haul laser-guided bombs into North Vietnam during Linebacker II.

Far left: Ordnance display. Early weaponry of the F-105D with electronics and cameras.

Above: An F-4E Phantom devoid of stores pylons shows off one of a number of camouflage schemes tried out after the end of the Vietnam war in order to render fighters harder to detect visually. This was the last St Louis built F-4.

carry a useful bomb load at high speed the Thunderchief was the primary weapon in TAC inventory for much of the war. There were some reservations that it might not be up to the task of hauling bombs in the hostile skies of the North, while being based in the hot and humid conditions of Thai bases. But the Thud stood up to both, writing yet another chapter in the history of Republic Aircraft, which ever since its Thunderbolt days has had a reputation for building strong airplanes – and the bigger, the better.

Apart from the B-52, which was perhaps the ultimate 'tactical' bomber but one outside the

scope of this book, in Korea the one fighter with which the US could if necessary take on the enemy in air-to-air combat was the Phantom.

This is not to say that the F-105 could not give a good account of itself if attacked – it could and did score a number of kills. Men with a sense of tradition in the fighter business actually envied the Thud driver; once free of his bomb load he could be more than a match for a MiG – because he had a gun to shoot with. Big, fast and glamorous though the Phantom was, coming to Vietnam combat with a string of performance records and undeniably built

Following pages: A Wild Weasel F-4G hung with the tools of its trade – the seeking out and destruction of enemy radar sites. For this it uses Shrike, Standard ARM, Maverick and HARM missiles, having pinpointed the target with Pave Spike. Unit here is the 37th TFW.

for nothing but combat, it had one drawback so far as the pilots were concerned. It had no gun.

Men who had been around fighters for some time recognised that in an F-4 they could out-distance just about anything else around, built either East or West of the fence. But in a fight, having to rely purely on guided missiles was a thing that took some getting used to. For one, nobody had ever gone to war in a fighter without a gun . . . however, the Navy reckoned missiles were enough and, after all, the F-4 carried at least four Sparrows and it could take another four Sidewinders on the wing racks.

Those privy to such things also knew that the Phantom's test program had included the use of guns in pods both under the fuelage and the wings, so at least these might be made available. But the fact of the Air Force's premier fighter having no gun was only part of the story. Launching from airfields in Thailand to be as near as possible to their targets in North Vietnam, fighter pilots had much more food for thought. Those who remembered might have recalled briefings on Luzon, Saipan, Foggia or sunny Wattisham, perhaps Kimpo or Taegu. Wherever or whatever the mission, the upshot was to go out and take on the enemy, without restrictions. Fighter pilots were there to beat the enemy.

But a briefing at Ubon, Udorn, Takhli or Korat were like few old hands had ever heard. They were amazed at the things they could not

do; they couldn't attack enemy airfields, were banned from flying over certain areas, of not going too far up near the border with China, they had to attack exactly what the frag order specified without any deviation and fly carefully pre-planned ingress and egress routes. Above all they were not to engage the enemy unless he attacked first.

They found that the war was run not by field commanders who were well placed to know what the latest state of play was, but by Washington. The President himself held all the aces, and yet seemed to be playing to lose. These were the Rules of Engagement. Not imposed by anyone else, like the UN, but by Lyndon B Johnson himself. An awful lot of questions were asked but few satisfactory answers were forthcoming. The US fighter pilot was in Thailand to fly cover for fighter bombers – preferably he would also haul bombs. He must not fight the enemy unless provoked.

Salvaging what there was left for them to do, fighter pilots went to war in Phantoms over North Vietnam to protect the strike force, hopefully by merely being there. It was seen by some as a sick joke perpetuated by some office-bound weenie, the last straw to break a fighter pilot's ego.

Re-inventing the Wheel

But things changed as time went on. The well-tested maxim that the best form of protection is to attack first was not completely overlooked.

F-4G

Powerplant: 2 × 17,900 lb thrust General Electric J79-15 afterburning turbojets

Dimensions – span 38 ft 5 in; length 63 ft wing area 539 ft³

Weights: empty 31,000 lb; loaded 60,360 lb

Performance: max speed: 1,500 mph at 35,000 ft; 910 mph at low level; ceiling 60,000 ft; range 2,660 miles

Above: F-4E of the 32nd TFS at Camp Amsterdam, Soesterburg in the Netherlands.

When the MiGs did start attacking US strike forces in April 1965, there were, naturally, combats. Thus the USAF in Vietnam began gradually the long process of re-inventing the wheel – to re-learn what every Mustang, Thunderbolt and Sabre pilot already knew, but also to graft onto those old rules the new ones more applicable to the fighter they were flying. Many Pilots or Aircraft Commanders before leaving the States had not had the time to explore the full extent of the Phantom's full flight envelope, to learn how to get the best out of an aircraft with an awsome amount of power.

When it came to shooting, the reliance on missiles was found to be optimistic. Designed to knock down a slow, non-manoeuvring bomber, both the Sidewinder and Sparrow were at times less than a fighter pilot's dream weapon. This fact, plus the one that says that your missile will just as happily home onto the exhaust of a J79 as a Tumanskii R-13, revealed that one of the Rules of Engagement (ROE) was undoubtedly more practical than it might have first seemed. Time and again visual identification brought US pilots positive results and reduced the possibility of shooting down friendlies rather than the bad guys. Mistakes did happen, but not that often.

Combats were invariably fought at distances that while starting off at useful missile ranges, often narrowed to be too close for missile effectiveness. Another factor was the speed at which combats took place and the lack of time for ideal positioning. The North Vietnamese were not out to give the Americans early warning of their presence in the air, and fought much as the MiG honchos had done over Korea. Their doctrine was the classic fast, surprise pass, open fire and get the hell out. Such tactics did not make aces and it was far from what their opposite numbers would have called 'sporty'. But it often worked, especially as bombers were the MiGs' first the foremost target.

North Vietnamese interceptions also had a desired-for 'knock on' effect. A MiG or two tearing through the trail formation of a Thud force could cause two, three or more USAF jocks to toggle their loads in order to manoeuver with the attackers. A Thud needed to drop the load in order to have a chance of fighting on even terms – but if Uncle Ho's men saw the bombs fall before the target was reached, their job was done. It was time to hightail it back to their sanctuary airfields, conserve the small force for the next US raid and if possible avoid any Phantoms – they too had their ROE.

These tactics galled red-blooded fighter pilots eager to see what the F-4 could do in anger. It soon became clear that to find out, a contingency plan was necessary.

Tricking the MiGs

On 2 January 1967, one of the most famous incidents to come out of the Vietnam air war was led by Robin Olds, a leading exponent of the F-4 Phantom and commander of the 8th Tactical Fighter Wing. On that day the famed 'Wolfpack' pulled off a ruse to bring the North Vietnamese MiGs up to fight – lure them into a decisive fighter-versus-fighter battle with no American fighter bombers to fudge the issue. With limited success it had been tried before, using a small number of Phantoms. What Olds and his fellow officers planned was a wing-strength mission with enough aircraft to take on the strongest enemy force.

The 8th Wing's Phantoms were F-4C

Left: A long production history sees many tests to extend an aircraft's flight and weapons capabilities. This F-4E is shown with an EROS electronic measuring device in one of the forward Sparrow AAM wells.

25

models, the first to be ordered by the Air Force. Not the first wing to go to Vietnam, the 8th was, however, the first of the 'permanent' F-4 wings to be based in Thailand and, with numerous squadron rotations, it would remain there up to and beyond the US involvement. It was also destined to return the largest number of MiG kills.

The force that was assembled for Operation Bolo was strong: 56 Phantoms and 16 F-104 Starfighters plus 24 F-105s to handle the then-vital task of radar suppression to guard the force from the electronic eyes of Fan Song radars which scanned North Vietnamese skies for the deadly SA-2 Guideline surface-to-air missiles. In support was the usual array of tankers and ECM aircraft to get the fighters into position and provide early warning of MiG activity.

To ensure as far as possible that the enemy would come up to fight, Olds and his pilots planned to fly a flight profile similar to a large force of F-105s. This was done by using Thud drivers' call-signs, speeds, altitudes, routes and jargon. This latter even included, for the benefit of any North Vietnamese ears, radio requests for en route fixes for Doppler radar position checks – which the Phantoms did not need, equipped as they were with an inertial navigation system. Everything possible was done to bait the trap: to all intents and purposes, what the enemy would detect would be nearly 100 American fighter bombers, out to

do considerable damage to a North Vietnamese ground target. It was a challenge to be taken up. . . .

All other aircraft which might otherwise venture over the North were grounded for the duration of the ruse mission. Olds therefore had a free hand – anything in the sky not recognised as an F-4 (and the smoke generated by a pair of J79s was often enought to mark a Phantom out from quite a distance) was fair game.

After some confusion caused by overcast skies, the Phantoms clashed with the MiGs when they were northwest of Hanoi. MiG-21s were up and Robin Olds' Phantom was the first to make contact. It took all his Sparrows and a pair of Sidewinders to despatch the Vietnamese fighter, which was seen to spin down like a falling leaf, on fire.

That was just for openers. The combats that followed saw the MiGs completely outclassed by the eager Americans. This was what it was about as far as they were concerned, at last a chance to prove what the F-4 could do. What it did do on that day was to shoot down seven MiG-21s for no loss. Everyone was elated, particularly as the adversaries had been '21s rather than the more numerous MiG-17. The MiG-21 was widely reckoned as more equal to the F-4 but – as always – much depended on the skill of the man at the controls.

It was a feature of the Vietnam War that the NVAF took periodic 'stand-downs' when activ-

Opposite: Variations in skin tones show up on these F-104s echeloned over barren desert terrain.

ity would be at a minimum and US air strikes were hardly challenged. A defeat like the Bolo operation was also followed by a period of absence, the implication being that the loss of pilots and aircraft had to be made good – and that took time. The North Vietnamese Air Force was never estimated to exceed more than 90 MiGs of all models at any one time, and there were relatively few men who were qualified to handle a fighter in combat.

On the other hand, the air force, integrated as it was with a formidable array of AA artillery of all calibers, plus a growing number of SAMs, did not need to be very large. Ground fire caused the majority of casualties among US aircraft throughout the war and this was widely reckoned to be formidable. Even 'down in the weeds' American fighter bombers were subject to curtains of small arms fire and although their aircraft were rugged and fast, the cost spiral continued to climb – in men as well as machines.

A pair of EF-111 Ravens; the USAF dedicated early warning aircraft, these machines are rebuilds of the F-111A.

Enter the 'Vark

Having embarked on a bombing campaign which was not backed up by ground troops capturing territory, the USAF tried to do in Vietnam the one thing that airpower has signally failed to do, short of using atomic weapons. By attempting to subdue a nation and break its will to fight primarily by bombing its industries, it had to have a virtual assurance that nearly every bomb hit its target and preferably, utterly destroyed it – quite a tall order. Not withstanding the various 'bombing pauses' imposed by Johnson to give the North Vietnamese the chance to say enough is enough and talk peace, such a task was all but impossible with the aircraft and methods used up to 1968 – with one exception. That exception seemed to be a very unlikely candidate to anyone who had followed the long, sad saga of TFX, which reached fruition in the shape of the General Dynamics F-111.

First flown on 24 December 1964 the YF-111A was supposed to be the forerunner of large production order for the Air Force and the Navy but technical problems – and politics – intervened. In attempting to meet a demanding specification and build in-commonality for widely differing roles in a single airframe, one that was also to incorporate a number of advanced features, the planners of TFX came unstuck. Potential excellence was masked then all but forgotten in a welter of public disquiet over costs, timescale, role, weapons and more costs. While the Vietnam War escalated, the one aircraft that might have made a big difference to the way the Air Force conducted operations lagged and languished. But the F-111 did not die.

By 1967 the USAF was in receipt of its first aircraft and the 'lemon' of press reports was about to prove its critics wrong – or right. On 17 July the CO of Detachment 1, 4481st Tactical Fighter Squadron, ferried an F-111A from Fort Worth to Nellis AFB to begin an operational conversion program for Air Force crews. These men would fly the most tested combat aircraft in history, find out what it was capable of and experience what pilots in another age also found out – that a big airplane is not necessarily the wrong one for the job it was designed to do. Those pilots of the past looked at the P-47 Thunderbolt and were awed by the fact that it took off at a little less than 15,000 lb gross weight. Two and one half decades later the F-111 crew noted that their fighter could load to 92,500 lb and take off without problems. And many people had said that a 60,000 lb F-4 was a little on the large side.

Left top: The USAF YE-111A prototype which made its first flight on 21 December 1974. Over the years the capability of the type has increased without major structural change,

Left: As a terrain-following bomber, the F-111 has few equals, even a decade and a half after first flight. This machine is in the markings of the 57th Fighter Weapons Wing.

Left below: Updated avionics and a revised engine inlet arrangement greatly increased the F-111's reliability. A 27th TFW aircraft, this D model carries Smart bombs and an AXQ-14 data link pod.

When is a Fighter not a Fighter?

In truth the F-111 never was a fighter, despite provision for an 'old fashioned' gun. Crammed with every electronic device that aerospace technology could provide, it was built to deliver a bomb load more than double that of the F-4. But the 'F' prefix was never changed and the difference, as the crews who flew it quickly found out, was that that kind of bomb load could be delivered accurately – more accurately than any other aircraft before it. It did not, like all the others, need much help to do the job; provided all its computers functioned as they should and there was a top-notch crew at the controls, the F-111, which was never officially named, but along the way collected the not-inappropriate handle 'Aardvark', could take out a target 1,800 miles from its base, alone. That was what the book said and some ten months later a handful of crews would find out when the Combat Lancer evaluation took six aircraft to Thailand.

As many would maintain, if luck is a necessary but intangible factor in the success of a warplane in action, the F-111 seemed at first to have a distinct lack of it. It came as no surprise to the critics when they read that in just under a month half the Combat Lancer force had been lost, presumably to enemy action.

That this had not been the case was more or less confirmed by the crew of the third machine downed who, unlike the men in the first

Heading for the weeds, an F-111 crew would configure their 'Aardvark' to full wing sweep to avoid enemy defences and 'ski' into their target.

Above: Head-on view of an F-111 shows the massive main landing wheels (a legacy from its intended Navy carrier role) and four fuel tanks on swivelling pylons.

Right: From above, the F-111 exhibits its full span wing position, large tail and side by side crew capsule, designed to break away in event of emergency.

two crashes (it had to be assumed), had managed to eject using the unique F-111 escape capsule. Designed to separate from the aircraft even at zero airspeed and zero height, this capsule enables the crew to leave the ship in relative comfort, parachutes deploying to bring it down to earth and provide a shelter until rescuers arrive.

The F-111 was still very new and it had not completed its Air Force test program before its combat debut. Given these circumstances, most aircraft might have suffered technical or operational difficulties and as tests in the US were soon to prove, it was not enemy action that had caused the losses over North Vietnam, but structural failure.

Examination of the airframe revealed that a control-valve rod in the tailplane power unit had failed, causing the left tailplane to swing to the limit of its negative travel, causing a sudden violent roll and pitch up. In this condition the aircraft was virtually uncontrollable – and at very low level the crew would have had no time to eject. Further probing was later to show that fatigue was present in the wing pivot fitting where a large tubular pin held the pivot to the wing box. There followed a costly inspection of every F-111 to determine the presence of any similar potentially lethal weakness in the structure. It solved the problems and after its first round of combat, the Aardvark would return to SE Asia.

F-111E

Powerplant: $2 \times 19,600$ lb thrust Pratt & Whitney TF30-3 afterburning turbofans

Dimensions: Span (fully spread) 63 ft; (fully swept) 31 ft $11\frac{1}{2}$ in; length: 73 ft 6 in; wing area 525 ft^3

Weights: (empty) 47,000 lb; (loaded) 92,500 lb

Performance: Max speed at 36,000 ft 1,450 mph; cruise speed 571 mph; ceiling 60,000 ft

Improved Phantoms

In May 1967 the 8th TFW was the first F-4 wing in SE Asia to take delivery of the next Air Force version of the Phantom, the D model. Lacking the under-nose IR sensor that was an external recognition feature of the F-4C, the new aircraft was considered as the first true Air Force model which, among other improvements, was wired to carry all the ordnance designed for that class of aircraft. Retrofitted with a radar homing and warning set, the F-4D soon had the under-nose sensor for the necessary aerials, making it virtually indistinguishable from the F-4C which continued to serve throughout the conflict.

Having thus far relied on Sparrow and Sidewinder AAMs, the F-4D introduced another weapon, the AIM-4D Falcon AAM. Not meeting with a great deal of success, this weapon was, like others that had offered to enhance USAF capability in combat, rarely used in action. Results obtained against drones and dummy targets over American firing ranges were often found to be unrepresentative of the conditions faced by front line pilots in a real war and, if nothing else, Vietnam showed that a whole new family of weapons and systems was needed if TAC was to prosecute this and future conflicts without prohibitive losses.

Of particular concern was the need to nullify any advantage the North Vietnamese had by using SAMs against US air strikes. It had been found that if early warning of an SA-2 launch was given it was possible for jet pilots to out-manoeuver the missiles, described by some pilots as giant, flaming telegraph poles.

That SAMs were dangerous was not a subject for discussion: pilots who experienced them said that being chased by a SAM was one of the most terrifying occurrences of their entire time in combat. In the light of such reports and USAF intitiated a far-reaching program to render the SAMs and their guidance system impotent. Chaff, the modern equivalent of the World War II ECM device Window, had been in use since the earliest days of the Rolling Thunder bombing campaign against the North. But blinding the radars for the duration of an air strike was only a temporary solution. What was really needed was a comprehensive system of finding, pin-pointing and if possible, destroying the radar so that however many SAMs the enemy managed to install to protect his factories, they would become so much useless metal. The fact that their radars were out did not prevent firings of course and when the Americans were able to achieve mass jamming, evidence of this was seen in random launchings of missiles in considerable numbers – but all the operators could then hope for was a lucky hit. It was a very expensive way to use such a weapon.

Under the generic name Wild Weasel, the USAF steadily developed its anti-radar capability, building on the results achieved by F-100 Super Sabres in the earliest days, and then from the more far-reaching operational experience of F-105F two seat Thuds, which did as much as any aircraft to prove that the SAM threat could be dealt with, not only by day, but during the hours of darkness as well.

The problem was that Thud attrition rate in Vietnam was high and the aircraft had finished its production run before the Vietnam war started. Conversion of single-seat F-105Ds into dual-seat F-105Fs and, later, Gs continued, but there were no new aircraft in the pipeline. On the other hand, as the F-4 had quickly carved itself an unassailable place in TAC inventory and was likely to remain in production for some years to come, it was important that if possible the Phantom should be modified to undertake this increasingly important role.

Unfortunately, the Wild Weasel F-4 program – the dedicated Wild Weasel aircraft, that is – took a good deal longer to perfect than expected and it was not until after the end of the war that the F-4G emerged. In the meantime the F-4 and other combat aircraft flew with podded ECM equipment and gradually the SAM threat was quantified. Strike forces went

out with a massive number of support aircraft to cover the bombers, and there were many more SAM firings than aircraft brought down. The danger was in no way eliminated, but it did not prevent the US from prosecuting the bombing campaign against the North which, by 1968, had devastated the country and destroyed much of its manufacturing industry – indeed some were moved to comment that the campaign continued through 1969–70 the outcome of the war might have been very different. As it was, the North Vietnamese turned a military defeat into a political victory with the 1968 Tet offensive. On 1 October 1968 Lyndon Johnson declared all of North Vietnam above the 17th Parallel 'off limits' to US airmen, and the three-year, two-month Rolling Thunder campaign came to an end.

Not that combat in South East Asia stopped; many more missions were to be flown before the 'next round', the May-October Linebacker campaign in 1972, but the headline-grabbing war of attrition provided a useful breathing space – for both sides. When US aircraft were seen again over Hanoi and its surrounding areas the war would be quite different and the price of continuing the war a good deal higher for Ho's regime than hitherto. The North had already seen – or more accurately not seen but heard – the F-111, experienced the advance in US missile technology when Shrike and Standard ARM anti-radiation missiles had been introduced to combat, and had lost heavily (in their terms) in air-to-air engagements with American fighters. Though they still hung on, it was a strange way for the North to win a war, by being outfought nearly every time it came to a stand-up fight.

Up to the 1968 bombing halt, USAF F-4s and F-105s had destroyed 86 MiG-17s and -21s in air combat for the loss of 15 F-4s and 21 F-105s. These figures compare favourably with the 156 Phantoms downed by AA and small-arms fire, and 12 which became the victims of SAMs.

While the majority of F-4 victories had fallen to AIM-7 Sparrow or AIM-9 Sidewinder AAMs, 14 May 1967 had seen the first MiG shoot-down by a Phantom using a gun, namely the SUU-16A. Enclosing a six-barrel Vulcan gun with rotating action, the pod was most usually slung from the centerline belly pylon of the F-4, although there were cases of pods being carried on wing racks – and one pilot took the lack of a built-in gun more personally than most and went to war with three 20 mm guns, two on wing hardpoints and one under the belly! It was certainly possible, but the aircraft must have been a little on the heavy side, especially when trying to turn with the nimble MiGs.

The foregoing figures show that the most dangerous element in the North's defense was ground guns. These also proved the hardest to deal with, as short of flying on the deck to knock them out by strafing and dropping anti-

Opposite: Wearing the distinctive blue and black starburst of the 318th FIS these F-15s appear to be flying near Mt St Helens.

personnel bombs (a highly risky business and one that was rarely undertaken) the USAF was left with trying to vary ingress routes to the targets as much as practicable and by switching altitudes. Trouble was that the en-route flight paths often had to be the same and therefore well known to the defenders. So great was the variety of hardware in North Vietnam that the threat extended from the bolt-action rifle held by a teenage girl crouching in a dike to radar-predicted AAA shells slinging steel thousands of feet into the air. This wall of steel had to be penetrated on most target runs and, perhaps ironically, the guns that were radar-controlled were the easiest to deal with.

Nothing could be done about the little lady in the dike, and her sisters, brothers, grandfathers and the rest of her comrades in arms. Radars could be blinded but the hand-held gunners became very adept at leading even the fastest jet aircraft and at least damaging it. After all, they had plenty of practise.

Eagles for the 80s

The life of a contemporary warplane is variable depending on its use, numbers procured and, sometimes, sales success around the world. Others spend their time purely in service with the host nation and do not find any other markets. But although actual lifespan is

Below: The similarity between the F-15 and the Navy's F-14 Tomcat can be appreciated from the side. From other angles the significant differences are apparent – but in capability the two principal US fighters of the 80/90s are close.

variable, the days when a warplane did not measure up to its design specification are all but over, as procurement costs are so astronomically high – and the design parameters so closely monitored that the end product is almost exactly to plan. One reason for this is that initial design studies take place far in advance of hardware and funding is secured years ahead, particularly in the case of the US. So it was that at the height of the Vietnam War, the Air Force requested funding for a fighter that would not take to the skies for seven years. This request, made in 1965, led to the F-15 Eagle, one of the most potent and costly fighters in current USAF inventory.

Submitted by McDonnell Douglas to meet the FX program in September 1968, the design was selected late the following year. What the company proposed was a twin-engined single-seater larger again than the Phantom and intended, as requested by the Air Force, to gain air superiority and deliver a significant amount of ordnance over long ranges – well over 2,500 miles with external tanks.

When it emerged the Eagle reflected the design thinking of the 1970s: twin fins, steeply raked air intakes with leading edge extension (LEX) to improve aerodynamic efficiency, the full suite of avionics – and a built-in gun. The F-16 and F-18 Hornet as well as the Navy's F-14 Tomcat perpetuated some of these features, but only the Tomcat had a variable-sweep wing. Only the F-16 relied on a single engine.

In the meantime, the tentative lull in the air war over North Vietnam began a period of keeping an eye on activity in the event that US air strikes were again sent into action above the 17th parallel. For this purpose the US employed a range of reconnaissance aircraft, among them the most potent in the world, the sinister SR-71 Blackbird. Designed to fly at altitudes up to 100,000 ft at speeds of 2,250 mph the Blackbird took its pictures with impunity, building on the mass of data already accumulated by the CIA and from 1969 by Strategic Air Command, which took over these operations during the course of the year. Also

Following pages: In many categories of military aircraft, the US enjoys a big advantage and while the gaps may narrow in other areas, in high altitude recon the SR-71 Blackbird reigns supreme.

available to the US was the Lockheed U-2, RF-101 Voodoo and Navy and Air Force reconversions of the Phantom. Under the new 'rules' the US would not reopen the bombing unless these flights were fired upon and then 'protective reaction strikes' would follow.

When the North Vietnamese did indeed attempt to stop overflights, the USAF sent its fighter bombers across the DMZ, but until 1972 the actions were relatively small scale, at least compared with the mass attacks of Rolling Thunder. A lot of action was still to be had in the South and in Laos, as the ground war continued to flare up. President Richard Nixon kept a close watch on developments and determined that the US involvement in Vietnam should close as soon as possible. But he was not at that time prepared to abandon South Vietnam to its fate. His 'peace with honor' pledge would be upheld.

While peace talks tentatively continued, the Air Force and other US forces were able to introduce a number of new weapons and systems, based on past combat experience. The Air Force at last took its 'custom-built' Phantom model, the F-4E, to Thailand – too late, it seemed for combat. No bombing of the North, no MiGs. It was a hard pill for the men of the 388th TFW to swallow. Having slogged along with the Thud during the roughest of the Thunder missions, part of the wing was now in the fighter business for real – but there was nobody to fight. The young turks had to bide

Opposite: In a stratosphere-grabbing climb, an F-14A of the 33rd TFW out of Eglin AFB, Florida making contrails.

their time. Combat was flown and their log books would reflect the fact. They knew that peace was not at hand. Not yet.

Many squadrons rotated back to the US during the 1969–71 time-frame and many men who had done their bit were not to return to Asia. Those that did would have better backing from American know-how and their missions, while still highly dangerous, would stand a better chance of success. For one, items like laser guidance for bombs had been introduced. And as previously mentioned, the anti-SAM technique had been thoroughly tested and brought to a pitch guaranteed to give the enemy a costly headache. Night attacks by high-speed jet aircraft had also matured, enabling many NVA/Viet Cong arms caches, transportation routes and missile sites to be destroyed in operations carried out under cover of darkness.

One of the early Eagles on the flightline with a representative warload of bombs and AAMs.

Linebacker

Nixon, frustrated at the antics of the North Vietnamese delegation at the Paris peace talks and then by being told that the enemy had started a major invasion of the South at the end of March 1972, vowed that this time the war would end on US terms. Militarily the North would be ruined, if that was what it took.

As the enemy made rapid advances in the South, the Air Force, Navy and Marines went back into action. On 6 April Nixon authorised Freedom Train, the resumption of strikes on the North. Before the month was out F-4Ds of the 432nd Tactical Reconnaissance Wing had destroyed three more MiGs. May saw the name of the game changed to Linebacker and on the 10th a series of air engagements re-

Below: An F-111 of the 20th TFW in typically sombre European-style tactical camouflage.

Below: England's own Aardvarks are the F-111E models belonging to the 20th TFW at Upper Heyford, Oxfordshire.

corded no fewer than 11 MiGs shot down – the best daily victory rate of the entire war.

During Linebacker II, the '11 day war' that on the home front all but ruined Hanoi's ability to fight, the F-111 went back for another crack at the world's most heavily defended targets. This time the results were spectacular. Not many pilots relished even the thought of trying to penetrate enemy territory at night in low cloud over mountains, and with the enemy trying his best to kill him. But F-111 jocks were a different breed. That is just what they did, not in wing or squadron strength, but alone. By September 1972 and 429th and 430th Squadrons were in Thailand, flying 'Lo' penetration missions with iron or cluster bombs. Just 16 bombs maximum per ship, delivered in the roughest weather and the darkest nights.

Such was the efficiency of the 'Vark's' system that the crew simply sat there and watched them go to work. Not even the target was seen. Trying their best to ignore the continual 'SAM activity' light show from the passive warning systems, the crew of the swing-wing skier – this being the nickname given to the F-111's flight profile – just carried on. Illuminating it was one thing, knocking a ground-hugging, very fast target quite another. In an ultimate hostility environment the NVA gunners rarely came close, which was unprecedented – and the more satisfying to talk about it later and watch the doubts finally fade.

By day, Linebacker II rounded out with an impressive 51 victories for US fighter pilots, offset by the loss of 17 F-4s and two F-105s, taking the year as a whole. One less than this total of Phantoms went down after SAM hits (again for the total period) while more than double the number succumbed to AAA/small arms fire – in this respect, little had changed and after the war it was determined that nearly 65 per cent of all USAF losses were attributable to enemy guns.

It was also said later that US combat victories should and could have been higher; such a belief is debatable given the ROE and other factors – perhaps the intangible will to win being replaced by a 'will to compromise' had too great an effect.

Some two months after Linebacker began on the other side of the Pacific, McDonnell Douglas flew the first of 20 development models of the F-15 Eagle. The St Louis concern which had produced the star of one war was now engaged on building a potential star for the one everyone hoped would not be the next. Along with the single-seat models would be two TF-15s both two-seaters intended primarily for the training task.

Winning Eagle

These aircraft were flown extensively and it soon became clear that in its new Eagle the USAF had a winner. Among other things it reflected time-honored penchant for the lone

Badge of the 57th Fighter Weapons Wing

Badge of the 27th Tactical Fighter Wing

Badge of the 366th Tactical Fighter Wing.

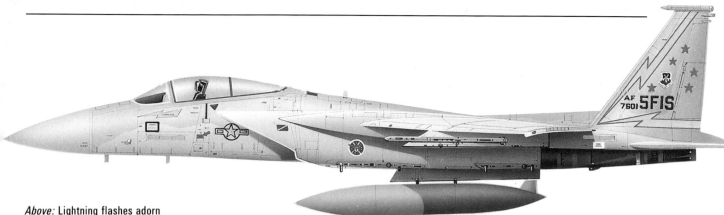

pilot and the Eagle was welcomed by many as a return to sanity. Authorisation to build 30 production aircraft came in March 1973.

Luke AFB was the location for handover of the first F-15 to the Air Force, the trainer since redesignated F-15B, on 14 November 1974. The following January TAC's 58th Tactical Fighter Training Wing took delivery of the Eagle and fittingly the first squadron to fly it operationally was the famed 555th TFS, 'Triple Nickel', the unit which had racked up 39 MiG kills over Vietnam and become the highest scorer.

What the 555th's pilots got was an extremely advanced piece of weaponry. Developments in cockpit management systems had been such that although representing a high work load for the single seat occupant, the Eagle was not difficult to fly. A new concept known as HOTAS – hands on throttle and stick – was born with the F-15. This meant that together with all vital data projected on the head-up display (HUD) in the form of alpha-numeric visuals, all the switches and buttons to operate the aircraft, communicate with other aircraft, check the radar state, sight the weapons and open fire, were grouped on either the throttle quadrant or the control column.

This system eliminated the need for a second seat but it did mean that the pilot had to spend a lot of his time looking out front. Three rear-view mirrors allowed him quick glances at what might be in his rear quarter, but generally his vision was not distracted by badly placed controls for a multitude of functions.

Powered by two P&W F100 engines of 23,930 lb of thrust, the F-15 can attain a maximum speed of 1,653 mph. Large, with a wingspan of just under 43 ft and nearly 64 ft long, the F-15 is nevertheless highly manoeuvrable, using its ailerons to roll at low speeds while the dogtoothed slab tailplanes and twin rudders take over this function entirely at speeds exceeding Mach 1. Low wing loading and high-energy manoeuvrability combined to give the Eagle unrivalled capability in the air superiority role yet still leave room for a useful load of ground-attack weapons.

The first wing to be fully Eagle-equipped was the 1st TFW at Langley AFB, Virginia, which went operational at the end of 1976. Second wing to fly the type was in an important part of the world – Europe. In 1977 Bitburg, in West Germany, echoed to the shattering roar of the F-15 when the 36th TFW began working up; having its best fighter in what might turn into a front line at some future date was seen as important by the USAF and the Eagle remains an integral part of the European commitment today.

There have been problems in a generally satisfactory program and a series of compressor stalls at low speeds, when the aircraft was at high altitudes, initially defied solution. The trouble was eventually traced to afterburner fuel flow. When the settings were changed at the point that a stall was sensed, fuel flow was reduced at the same time the AB nozzles were opened. This operation took place automatically. There were further problems and delays in deliveries of engines and time between trimming to operate at lower temperatures dropped to an unacceptable low rate of readiness for the Eagle force.

But these problems were solved and the F-15 remains at the very pinnacle of Air Force readiness to defend the Free World against any threat. It is true to say that today's Air Force pilot is better equipped and better trained to fly an ultra-capable aircraft than at any time previously. Although the current generation of fighters has not seen actual combat in American hands, both the Eagle and

Below: A plain, early production F-15 test fires a Sparrow AAM, one of the first such weapons cleared for the Eagle's use. From Sparrows and Sidewinders the Eagle went on to haul vast quantities of stores, at least in the 'mud mover' role.

Right: A gentle pull on the stick and up and over she goes, like a bat out of hell. A few fighters can keep up with the Eagle — luckily, they're all on our side!

Following pages: The first F-15C climbing out of Edwards AFB in August 1983 carrying Fast Pack fuel pallets, inert Sidewinders, and Mk 82 low drag bombs.

Fighting Falcon have been sold to Middle East customers. That area of the world is almost guaranteed to find work for military forces and figures released by the Israeli Air Force include the fact that during the Lebanon invasion IAF F-15s scored an incredible 86 victories without loss, the score including a Syrian MiG-25. Further success was achieved by the Royal Saudi Air Force in June 1984 when two Iranian F-4s out over the Gulf on an anti-shipping tanker strike were intercepted by RSAF F-15s, and shot down by a single AIM-7 launched from each Eagle.

For the American Eagle pilot, war is a sweat-drenched, mind-boggling, eye-straining, high-G turning match with his own people, kills being registered electronically by sensors as he flies to the limits on a constant round of air combat manoeuvring training. Whether it be a squadron mission or the ultra-realistic tussle with the Aggressors over the Nellis ranges, the objective is the same. Each man must give of his best and show that he can continue to hack the stresses imposed on him, both mentally and physically. This deadly serious training to fight came about as a result

Left: Eagle built for two is the F-15B. This example hones the principles upheld by the 555th TFS, the famed 'Triple Nickle' squadron.

of the showing of USAF fighters over Vietnam. When it was over, the results of all the MiG engagements were minutely analysed with the intention of creating a new breed of fighter pilot. Unlike his counterpart of the early 1960s, the fighter jock of the 80s and 90s would know his aircraft and its capabilities intimately, be able to fly it to the very extremes of the flight envelope and perhaps most important of all understand what he himself would do if the training ever turned into the real thing.

Along with the products at the Navy's Top Gun school, set up for a similar training purpose, the Air Force fighter pilot tends these days to be just that. There is not much interest in the 'multi-role aircraft' as the Air Force would rather have variants of the same design tailored to the ground-attack task and keep the air-to-air separate. This makes sense as the two tasks have very different requirements –

and fighter pilots are totally in agreement on this point!

Many pilots also prefer to fly in the more realistic arena of Europe than the clear skies of Nevada. A posting to USAFE is much sought after, as a NATO assignment brings in a whole new element to the curriculum. For one thing, there are all the various types of European aircraft likely to be met during exercises and exchange visits, plus the fact that different air forces have a variety of tactics and methods, all of which offer a challenge. Then there is, as always, the weather. Clear skies are fine, but 'low vis' conditions do hold the attention, as do the airspace rules that keep Europe's high volume of air traffic in order. Understandably, if Germany does one day turn into the front line and Americans are asked to help, fighter pilots want to become familiar with their operational area well before any shooting starts.

Below: An F-15A, also in service with the 555th TFS when the parent 58th TTW was at Luke AFB.

Electric Jet

Representing the other element of the current USAF fighter force is the General Dynamic F-16 Fighting Falcon. A totally different machine to the F-15, it is far smaller, more modern and reflects the rapid advances in avionics, cockpit ergonomics and airframe design in the last decade. It is also interesting to note that the F-16 represents a change in US attitudes toward the light-weight, small fighter. Traditionally American fighters have been large and complex (some would say overly so) and in marked contrast to the requirements of European and other air arms around the world; but paradoxically a significant number of these countries actually got into the modern fighter business by ordering the Northrop F-5 Freedom Fighter.

Designed in the 1950s when there arose a much-heralded trend away from the huge and increasingly costly fighters being produced in the US, the F-5 was a bold step toward meeting this demand. But Northrop was obliged to weather a long and expensive battle to get its little single-seater accepted by the Department of Defense, even though it was not intended for US use but for sale through the Military Aid Program to foreign nations. However, any US aircraft does have to have a DOD

Left: F-16A Fighting Falcons of the 120th FIG, Montana ANG known as the 'Big Sky Country' according to the fin banner.

Right: The first F-5F Tiger II was the two-seat model of the updated, radar equipped fighter that followed on from the F-5A.

Inset: Fast-turning T-38 Talon in the colours of the Thunderbirds. The team flew the little 'White Rocket' for more than 400 shows.

One of the international best sellers of the Military Assistance Program, the Northrop F-5E has been operated by some 20 countries.

seal of approval and there was much opposition to the swing away from established doctrine. Anything that smacked of 'economy' seemed at that time to be anathema to the US military establishment.

Northrop eventually convinced the doubters that it did indeed have the right fighter for countries whose military defense budgets were modest. The Californian company fended off the larger concerns which were constantly trying to sell 'limited capability' versions of the hot US fighters and showed that the F-5 offered reliability from a new airframe, ease of maintenance and lower operating costs – all factors that were well understood by the potential customers.

Success came after Northrop had produced the T-38 Talon trainer for the Air Force and which, from March 1961, became the backbone of Air Training Command. Many thousands of F-5A single seaters, F-5B dual control trainers and subsequently, the more potent F-5E fighters, saw service throughout the world. The USAF itself operated the F-5 when 12 A models were beefed up for combat evaluation in Vietnam under the codename Skoshi Tiger. These aircraft arrived at Bien Hoa in South Vietnam on 23 October 1965 and flew their first combat missions the same day.

This debut did not however herald widespread use of the Freedom Fighter by the USAF; the evaluation was primarily for the

benefit of South Vietnam, an important customer for the type. To the SVNAF it was recognition that its pilots were capable of taking a modern jet type into combat on their own account.

The F-5 was destined to become the spearhead of the South Vietnamese Air Force and was, along with the Cessna A-37 and B-57 (the latter eventually being crewed by Vietnamese but remaining under USAF control), some compensation for the Phantoms that had been requested. This was denied, mainly on the grounds that in Vietnamese hands Phantoms might just have circumvented the carefully worked out planning for the war's conduct. Another factor was the lack of skilled Vietnamese personnel to service such a modern type, not to mention a lack of the necessary support organisation.

The American pilots handed their F-5As over to their allies and were not directly associated with the Northrop fighter until the Vietnam War had run its course. By 1975, when the South faced irreversible defeat, 25 F-5s were flown to Thailand and were later shipped back to the States. These aircraft, for which the USAF had no immediate use, were stored along with other embargoed F-5s intended for Ethiopia, pending disposal.

Enter the Aggressors

In the event, these machines were quickly refurbished and not without a touch of irony, flown as the 'enemy' in a new program of dissimilar air combat manoeuvring, or the 'Aggressors' as the role they undertook became widely known, following activation of the 64th Fighter Weapons Squadron at Nellis AFB on 10 October 1972. Only later redesignated the Aggressors, the 64th pioneered an entirely new concept in fighter pilot training. Such men have never looked back and they still fly to the limits to evade Northrop F-5s that look like MiGs (at least to a radar) and fly very much as the men of the Soviet Union are known to do.

While the F-5 is an integral part of the training syllabus and the F-15 represents perhaps the opposite end of the spectrum, the wide acceptance of the F-16 particularly by Israel and NATO air forces, parallels the F-5 saga more than a little. A directive from the DOD started the ball rolling in 1970. A call was made for innovative aviation programs for what was termed 'prototyping concept' studies. These were aimed at selecting the right aircraft for the US services, at the right price, the winner being decided in prototype fly-off competition. Northrop and General Dynamics were the main beneficiaries of the initial $100 million funding, with the balance going to engine manufacturers Pratt & Whitney and General Electric. The money brought two prototype aircraft from each manufacturer, the Northrop YF-17 Cobra and GD's YF-16.

Opposite: After flying Thuds and Phantoms in Vietnam, the 388th TFW is currently an F-16 wing. In 1981 these A model Fighting Falcons were photographed on a sortie out of Hill AFB, Utah.

Now the attitude to the lightweight, agile fighter had completely changed: Vietnam had shown that it was sound practise to have air superiority vested in a substantial number of cheaper, perhaps less technically capable, fighters than a limited number of big, complex and expensive machines. And there was no reason why such a fighter would not be attractive to the Navy as well.

The Striking Cobras

In fact, nine companies responded to the fighter proposal but it was the new aircraft that attracted the most attention. Some, including Lockheed's, were updates or modifications of existing designs which did not find much favour. The choice narrowed to Northrop and GD, the former's very striking Cobra having been designed as an F-5 successor.

When the YF-16 was selected as the USAF's new fighter, the Northrop Cobra found another avenue for success. It became the forerunner of the McDonnell Douglas F-18 Hornet and the two companies underwent a marriage of convenience to collabroate on this huge Navy program.

There was more behind the Air Force's decision to 'go light-weight', as foreign sales were looming attractively in the early 1970s. NATO air forces in need of new equipment baulked at the costly support requirements – not to mention unit price – of investing in the F-15, but they were very interested in something smaller and better tailored to their defense budgets. With numbers such as at least 350 aircraft (for Norway, Belgium, Denmark and Holland) being talked of, it was small wonder that the US lightweight fighter represented the 'sale of the century' if a European deal came off.

The YF-16 made its maiden flight on 20 January 1974 and made an impressive debut; the aircraft was a radical departure to anything in service before. The fuselage shape was dictated by a need to enhance lift at high angles of attack and to accommodate a gun and additional fuel, while the outer wing was of more conventional straight delta configuration with no less than eight stores stations across the 31-foot span, including pylons at each tip for AAMs. Each wing incorporated hinged leading and trailing edge flaps – the latter doubling as flaperons – for good combat manoeuvrability. A massive 23,840 lb thrust P&W F1000 afterburning turbofan propelled the F-16 at speeds up to 1,350 mph at 40,000 ft. More importantly, the aircraft does not trade much weight for each pound of thrust. At 23,357 lb loaded it can be seen that the F-16A offers over a pound of thrust for every pound of weight.

It is in the cockpit area that the most startling advances have been made over fighters past. For a start there is but one strengthening frame to mar an otherwise clear bubble – the nearest the modern fighter has come to the open cockpits of 1914 – and a good deal more comfortable! Pilot comfort is about as good as it can be, with a reclining seat and side-stick controller for the fly-by-wire electrically-signalled flight controls – one reason why the US fighter pilot community has all but abandoned the official name 'Fighting Falcon' for the more catchy 'Electric Jet'.

The Air Force gave the go-ahead for full scale development of the F-16 in January 1975, emphasising that this meant procurement of a two-seater (F-16B) and an extensive ground-attack capability for the A model as an alternative to the pure fighter. Part of this latter requirement was reflected in the choice of

Below: Tuckin' in close. The boys from Montana's 120th Group are, like the rest of the Air Guard, a potent second-line force.

Falcon by the four air forces already mentioned, NATO's task being predominantly concerned with ground attack.

With the European order announced in June 1975, the F-16 also secured a multi-national production complex and the following month the USAF ordered its first six F-16As and two B models, the forerunners of an intended buy of 1,184 As and 204 Bs. In anticipation of such numbers, GD designed-in a high degree of

adaptability and as production got into gear the aircraft was strengthened to carry EO/FLIR and laser pods and the central computer and avionics suite were changed to incorporate improvements. To offset the additional weight a graphite/epoxy tail plane, larger than that originally fitted, was developed, and further changes are in the offing. There is every indication that the outstanding F-16 will accommodate them all with little noticeable effect on its superlative performance.

Above: General Dynamics Test Pilot Neil Anderson n the cockpit of an early F-16. Note the barrel cooling slots of the 20mm gun.

Above and right: Three-tone camouflage sets off the black wolf's head of 8th TFE F-16As based in Korea as part of PACAF. The head-on view shows the small frontal area of the Falcon and the strong undercarriage units. Sidewinders are carried on the wingtips of most fighter Falcons.

Plan view of the Falcon gives an idea of how much the pilot is able to see from the best cockpit view to be had. Wing planform also gives excellent roll characteristics.

F-16A

Powerplant: 1 × 23,840 lb thrust Pratt & Whitney F100-200 afterburning turbofan

Dimensions: Span 31 ft; length: 47 ft 7 in; wing area 300 ft³

Weights: (empty) 15,137 lb; (loaded) 23,357 lb

Performance: Max speed: 1,350 mph at 40,000 ft; 915 mph at sea level; ceiling 50,000 ft plus. Range: (max ferry) 2,415 miles.

Combat in the 80s

Below: 'Blooded' in action during the Tripoli raid, the EF-111A proved worth its high investment in sophisticated electronics. For the standard F-111s the Eldorado Canyon strike was the third taste of combat.

Although there have been a number of recent incidents of US fighters opening fire on adversaries during the course of combat missions, most of these have fallen to the Navy and all have centered on the troubled Middle East. Not until 14 April 1986 did the USAF participate by mounting a controversial raid on the Libyan capital, Tripoli.

Specific targets in and around the city were allocated to 18 F-111Fs stationed at Mildenhall, Suffolk, home of the 48th TFW. The raid launched just after 1800 hours, the main force being accompanied by six spare 'Varks, supported by KC-135 tankers. Three additional EF-111A Ravens, with two spares, left Upper Heyford, Oxfordshire, at around the same time, these machines being part of the 42nd Electronic Countermeasures Squadron.

Due to diplomatic denial of land over-flying rights, the force headed out over the Atlantic,

rounded Portugal and continued on into the western Mediterranean. While off Gibraltar the crews received their final orders that the mission was to go ahead as planned.

In the target area the USAF force was joined by aircraft of the Sixth Fleet, assigned to other Libyan targets. After military barracks, believed to have harbored Col Gadaffhi's terrorist training school, the commando training school at Sidi Bilal, the military side of Tripoli Airport and targets in the harbour, the F-111s dropped 2,000 lb laser guided bombs. For the loss of a single aircraft which crashed into the sea after the strike the F-111 force otherwise received little damage from the Libyan AAA and SAM launches after the initial surprise of the attack had passed. With Navy aircraft attacking at the same time, it would be difficult for the layman to state exactly who hit what. Predictably the Western media played up civilian casualties to the full, but the USAF's post-strike overflights of Tripoli undoubtedly revealed much fuller details than have as yet been released for general consumption.

Despite US indications that the raid would be followed by others if there were any further Libyan-inspired or executed attacks on US personnel, the Air Force was not called upon again. While it was the third time that the F-111 had been in action after the two Vietnam deployments, Operation Eldorado Canyon marked the combat debut of the Raven, the dedicated ECM version; the three EF-111s that penetrated Libyan airspace returned safely.

Mainstay of the 'T-birds' for many years, the 'Hun' also gave the USAF maximum return for its investment, taking it into the supersonic age. This F-100D model seen in '60s show colours, bowed out for the F-4 in 1969.

Thunderbirds

Officially known as the 3600th Air Demonstration Squadron, the USAF Thunderbirds aerobatic team has been an inspiration to fledgling fighter pilots since 1 June 1953. On that date seven officers, 15 NCOs, six F-84G Thunderjets and a single T-33A began a tradition. From those small beginnings at Luke AFB, Arizona, the Thunderbirds have flown their striking red, white and blue fighters to the delight and admiration of millions, both throughout the USA and around the world. Maintained by the Air Force primarily as a boost to recruiting, the team has, unlike most other world-class aerobatic formations, been mounted on the latest front-line fighters, so that, with hand on heart, USAF officers can tell any youngster in an air show crowd that if he matches up, he too could fly an airplane exactly like the ones he sees performing highly elaborate and exciting manoeuvers across the sky.

Only once when even the USAF was forced to break this tradition due to the world fuel crisis, did the Thunderbirds fly a trainer. In 1974 the team traded the Phantom, arguably their most impressive mount ever, for the diminutive T-38. Flying from Nellis, home to the 'T-birds' since 1956, the Talon was to bring one of the saddest periods when four aircraft crashed to terminate the 1982 show season before it had even begun.

Prior to the Talon and F-4, the team had

flown the F-84F Thunderstreak, F-100C and D models of the Super Sabre before passing briefly onto the F-105B in 1964. More crashes saw the team back on the F-100D to round out that season before a change was made to the F-4E in 1969.

Crashes and the loss of pilots invariably lead to discussion about disbanding aerobatic teams – not only in the US but anywhere else that the worst happens – but the T-Birds weathered the 1982 tragedy and went on to the F-16 in 1983. En route to the Falcon, an F-15 was painted in Thunderbirds' colours and although it looked every inch the part, there was no intention to form the team on the Eagle.

Smaller and with its legendary manoeuvra-

Above: Two seats gave the mighty Thud a very important new lease of life during the Vietnam war. Uncomfortable though it was for the back seat 'Bear' the F-105F performed the vital radar suppression role and helped write a new chapter in air warfare.

bility, the Falcon appears to be one of the best aircraft for this demanding job that has ever been selected. As important to the Air Force is the fact that the Fighting Falcon is of course a first-line type.

Electronic-eye Fighters

As indicated previously, the end of the Vietnam War saw a whole range of new combat techniques emerge from the smoke of battle to become an increasingly important part of the USAF for decades to come. Few were as important as the dedicated systems platform for the anti-radar war, the Wild Weasel. Today much of that duty is still undertaken by one of the remaining USAF Phantom models, the F-4G, a highly refined version of the F-4E.

The F-4G was in fact Wild Weasel 5, following the F-100 and F-105 which had so ably handled this task during the Vietnam war. No 4 Weasel was the F-4C and a pair of F-4Ds. Two squadrons, the 81st and 67th, were formed using these modified aircraft, the former going to Germany to introduce the mission requirement to NATO, while the 67th winged its way to Okinawa and thence to Thailand in time for Linebacker II.

The 67th performed well in combat and although its aircraft carried the Shrike anti-radar air-to-ground missile, the Phantom could not then be fitted with the larger, more able Standard ARM – anti-radiation missile. It was a hard enough task just finding room for the assorted electronic detection equipment in the short-nosed Phantom's already crowded airframe; homing, launch warning and detectors in the low, mid and high transmission frequencies were just some of the additionals and the F-4C had external aerials to mark it out from standard squadron fighters. Inside the cockpit, panels were modified to take the 'scopes of a threat display panel and receiver display.

Lack of a Standard ARM missile did not hamper Wild Weasel Phantoms during the closing stages of Linebacker, and much success was achieved with Shrike and old-fashioned iron free-fall bombs – once the target was identified, any weapon could theoretically destroy it. The difference was that the special missiles homed right onto it. Shrike was limited in that the parent aircraft had to fly close in to the enemy radar, the missile having only limited guidance. Standard ARM had a powerful seeker head which guided onto the radar irrespective of the direction the aircraft was flying.

For the Weasel task the F-4E airframe was much more suitable; technicians stripped out all equipment not essential to the anti-SAM role and put in an APR-38 Radar Warning and Attack System comprising an IBM receiver to feed threat information to a Texas Instruments computer, which then indicates the threat. The system included a GE lead computing gunsight/head up display, a radar homing and

An elegant view of a YF-17 trying to keep station with the camera ship during a test flight.

warning system for specific signals, and a data tape recorder.

The APR-38 system was installed on 116 converted F-4Es, which took the designation F-4G. The suffix had been used briefly before by the Navy and only involved a small number of aircraft, so it seemed convenient to take it up once more with the new USAF Phantom. To make way for the system's receivers, the F-4E's M61A-1 20 mm gun was removed and once again the Phantom relied entirely on missile armament. These included the Texas Instruments AGM-45C Shrike; GE AGM-78D Standard ARM; Texas Instruments AGM-88A HARM (High Speed Anti-Radiation Missile) and Hughes AGM-65 Maverick. In addition, the F-4G carried Westinghouse ALQ-119 and -131 counter-measures pods.

As it remains the one aircraft in USAF inventory fully committed to the Weasel role, the F-4G will be around for some years yet, as will other Phantoms, including the RF-4C reconnaissance aircraft. Older versions of the aircraft are also operated by the Air National Guard and USAF Reserve force although the F-4 is no longer the TAC spearhead it once was, the support it provides is invaluable.

Strike Eagle

If the USAF has recently placed much emphasis on the prowess of its fighter pilots in their ultra-capable aircraft, training ceaselessly to handle any air combat situation that might develop in the future, fighters are still obliged, despite equal enthusiasm from bombers such as the B-1 and the stealth B-2 and F-117 stealth fighter, to be equipped for the 'mud mover' ground-attack role. Most fighter types have traditionally had a secondary ground-attack role but the size of the Air Force in recent years has meant that the two tasks can be separated. Also, for the first time in its history, there is the purpose-built A-10 Thunderbolt II intended for nothing but the strike task. Armed with a formidable array of bombs and a mighty built-in cannon, an A-10 would be equally effective against tanks and soft-skinned vehicles – but there is a place for the higher performance fighter able to deliver a hefty punch, clear the battlefield and take on enemy aircraft en route back to base.

While this view of the multi-role aircraft is not whole-heartedly accepted in some quarters and must, even to a limited degree, result in a compromise, it is sound practise to see just what an airframe can carry without drastic modification – after all improvisation may still be needed, even in the highly orchestrated war scenarios of the future. These do not always turn out to be quite as imagined, so it is sensible to have aircraft and helicopters cleared to carry ground-attack weapons even in what might appear on the face of it to be strictly an air-to-air situation. And there is also the foreign customer; fighters such as the F-15 and F-16 have sold extremely well around the

Far right: A picture to gladden the heart of the company executives catches Eagles in their natural environment. The terrain is Alaskan, the unit the 43rd TFS.

Hill Air Force base brood is a flight of F-16As from the 388th Wing.

world to air forces that do not have the luxury of different types of aircraft configured for specialised purposes. A new way to accommodate ordnance, an improved missile launch rack (possibly one that doubles the number previously carried without undue weight penalty), a new reconnaissance/camera pack that turns a fighter into a fast surveillance aircraft, ECM equipment that also extends the role for certain missions – the list is very long indeed. Innovations in aerospace 'goodies' whether they be integral or the 'bolt-on' variety are always around the corner, and the USAF has never been backward in funding programs that offer to extend the capability of an existing type.

For this reason, the 'basic' modern fighter usually starts life as a single seater, flying in

Above: An F-16A illustrating the TAC two-tone grey/blue scheme.

relatively 'clean' condition without racks, pods or pallets to mar its lines. The next quite logical step is to introduce the two-seater to undertake a training role, there being few substitutes for a student pilot to get the feel of the front line fighter he hopes to fly from the rear seat first.

After the trainer, the field is wide open; if the type in question is chosen to stay in service for any length of time – and these days development costs are so high that this is virtually a foregone conclusion – then we see the ground-attack variant, the PR model, a reconnaissance conversion, and so on. Today's first line American fighters are no exception to this rule and both the Eagle and Fighting Falcon have flown with the whole spectrum of

additions adaptable to their class, weight and performance.

The Eagle, for example, now comes in four models; the A (fighter) and B (trainer) have already been mentioned but in addition there is the F-15C and D, respective updates of the A and B models. Each carries an extra 2,000 lb of fuel, another UHF radio, a better radar which extends target lock-on to ranges of 50 miles, a generally strengthened airframe with a tougher landing gear, and a more reliable ejector seat. In reverse of the usual procedure, the external engine nozzle flaps – 'turkey feathers' to the front line people – were removed. This not only cut maintenance time – but no less than $1,200 for each of the 17 flaps fitted to the Eagle. In the increasingly cost-conscious Air Force, this was a considerable saving when taken 'across the board'.

The F-15 C and D models can also carry the McDonnell-developed 'Fast Pack', an ingenious pallet that conforms to the aircraft's fuselage contours and contains no less than 4,875 lb of fuel, reconnaissance and ECM sensors. A Fast pack boosts the Eagle's range considerably and is a relatively cheap way to achieve this ongoing requirement (for any fighter), but without the previous penalty of high drag from ever-larger drop tanks and ferry tanks on external pylons.

Changes 'under the skin' are legion and probably far more numerous than anything that is added on externally. In what is perhaps the fastest-growth area in aerospace today, the F-15 is only one aircraft type that has benefitted from micro-processor-based aircraft management systems which increasingly are able to handle more and more of the actions needed to fly the ship, irrespective of whether these were previously undertaken by the pilot, or (more commonly) older technology. Automation is definitely the name of the game.

Let Chips do the work

Putting in a 16-bit microcomputer with an 8,5 K memory to juggle a gas generator and afterburner control unit in the F-15 pushed up speed, acceleration, take off roll, time to climb, removed any restrictions on throttle operation and enabled air-starts to be made at 200 kts at 10,000 ft, 50 kts slower than previously. Few more convincing arguments need be made for cockpit automation, which continues to advance this particular aspect of fighter operations.

In 1983 the USAF funded a $274.4 million program for upgrades to the F-15's radar, central computer and armament control systems as part of the on-going multi-stage improvement program (MSIP). Among other increases in the Eagle's capability, this gave better radar ranging, higher computer processing speed and memory improvement, and allowed for carriage of the new weapons, including the Hughes-120 AMRAAM. In total this MSIP effectively extended not only the F-15's reliability immediately but allowed for future weapons and systems to be incorporated. Added on production lines, the new features are also retrofitted on older F-15s.

A similar updating path has been followed by General Dynamics for the F-16 although generally speaking the Falcon flies more in the air defense (fighter) role than on ground attack. The improved F-16C flew for the first time on 19 June 1984, with deliveries to the USAF later that year. The updating was similar to that carried out on the Eagle and for a similar purpose.

'Stretchability' is also on the cards with any fighter program likely to have a long service life, not only because that life can extend but

Right: Plain Jane Eagle a good few 'angels' above the daily cares of man. Clean lines and lack of equipment to mar the pilot's cockpit rear view are obvious.

Inset: All the well-trained US fighter pilot needs – the 'Electric Jet' armed with missiles and a gun.

also as a safeguard should military budgets be reduced. Currently the US is having to look closely at its defense spending, following the election of George Bush to the White House. The legacy of a large deficit has already brought cutbacks and cancellations in future hardware, but the fighter procurement side has remained intact.

Looking to the future, the F-16 may well prove to be the winner of the USAF program to find a fighter that costs less than an F-16 cur-

An early F-16B shows about the maximum load the two-seater can lift and still have the edge.

rently does. GD has entered a revised Fighting Falcon, the SC model, and a figure of 300 aircraft has been quoted as the initial buy.

Even more dramatic is the STOL Eagle. A proposal has been put forward by McDonnell Douglas to convert the 80s interceptor into a 90s and beyond short-runway operator. It achieves this by the addition of shoulder-mounted canards and rectangular engine exhaust nozzles. The canards increase lift and the box exhausts deflect air downwards to shorten the take off. On landing, reverse thrust aids braking, giving a landing run reduction of one third or so – from 3,000 ft to 1,000 ft in dry conditions and from 10,000 ft to 1,200 ft in the wet. Developed in conjunction with Pratt & Whitney, the concept has been around for some time and whatever the final configuration is, it is certain that the F-15s around at the end of the century will once again reflect a quantum leap in the march of progress, as it apertains to the American fighter business.

USAF FIGHTER INVENTORY, 1989

Type	Number in service
F-111A/D/E/F	325+
EF-111A Raven	42
F-15E Eagle	392[R]
F-15A/B Eagle	420+
F-15C/D Eagle	469[R]*
F-16A/B	735+
F-16C/D	1936[R]*
F-4C/D/E Phantom	1200+
RF-4C Phantom	325+
F-5E/F Tiger II	80+
Lockheed F-117A	49
A-7D/K Corsair II	380+

*Delivery of these types is now in progress.
[R]Required number, but not all aircraft are ordered.

AIR COMMAND STRUCTURE FOR USAF OPERATIONS
The main USAF AFB's outside Europe are shown below

TACTICAL AIR COMMAND

TAC HQ:
Langley AFB, Virginia

Air Defence TAC:
Langley AFB, Virginia

21st Air Division
(Hq. Hancock Field, N.Y.)

23rd Air Division
(Hq. Tyndall AFB, Fla.)

24th Air Division
(Hq. Malmstrcm AFB, Mont.)

25th Air Division
(Hq. McChord AFB, Wash.)

26th Air Division
(Hq. Luke AFB, Ariz.)

Air Forces Iceland
(Keflavik NAS, Iceland)

USAF Air Defense Weapons Center
(Hq. Tyndall AFB, Fla.)

9th Air Force
(Hq. Shaw AFB, S.C.)

USAF Southern Air Division
(Hq. Howard AFB, Panama)

USAF Tactical Fighter Weapons Center
(Hq. Nellis AFB, Nev.)

USAF Tactical Air Warfare Center
(Hq. Eglin AFB, Fla.)

12th Air Force
(Hq. Bergstrom AFB, Texas)

831st Air Division
(George AFB, Calif.)

832d Air Division
(Luke AFB, Ariz.)

833rd Air Division
(Holloman AFB, N.M.)

836th Air Division
(Davis-Monthan AFB, Ariz.)

PACIFIC AIR FORCES

HQ:
Hickham AFB, Hawaii

326th Air Division
(Hq. Wheeler AFB, Hawaii)

5th Air Force
(Hq. Yokota AB, Japan)

313th Division
(Hq. Kadena AB, Japan)

314th Air Division
(Hq. Osan AB, Korea)

13th Air Force
(Hq. Clark Ab, Philippines)

ALASKAN AIR COMMAND

HQ:
Elmendorf AFB

Eilson AFB

79

Acknowledgements

The publishers are grateful to manufacturers for many of the illustrations in this book, to *Pilot Press* (pages 6, 7, 8, 9, 10, 11, 12, 24, 28, 31, 38, 42, 44, 47, 50, 53, 54, 58, 62, 67, 74, 75, 77, 78) *Jerry Scutts* (pages 13, 14, 16, 17, 18, 19, 20, 22, 27, 35, 40, 55, 56, 60, 61, 63, 66, 68, 69). *Octopus Books Ltd* (pages 2, 30, 32-33, 36, 44, 45, 46, 48, 49, 52, 64-65, 73, 77).